BURLESQUE

MICK EVANS

Cinnamon Press
:: small miracles from distinctive voices ::

Published by Cinnamon Press
Meirion House,
Glan yr afon,
Tanygrisiau
Blaenau Ffestiniog,
Gwynedd, LL41 3SU
www.cinnamonpress.com

The right of Mick Evans to be identified as author of this work has been asserted by him in accordance with the Copyright, Designs and Patent Act, 1988. Copyright © 2016 Mick Evans
ISBN: 978-1-78864-036-7
British Library Cataloguing in Publication Data. A CIP record for this book can be obtained from the British Library.

Designed and typeset in Palatino by Cinnamon Press.
Cover design by Jan Fortune.

Cinnamon Press is represented in the UK by Inpress Ltd and in Wales by the Welsh Books Council

Acknowledgements

Sincere thanks are due to the following:
Jane Belli for her inspiration and setting me on the path; Ted Clarke for guidance in the world of the Punch and Judy man; Sian Hughes for her insistence that Punch had legs; Dominic and everyone at the Queen's; Dinefwr Poets for their friendship and support.
Especial thanks are due to Jan Fortune for her unstinting labours, kindness and encouragement, and everyone at Cinnamon; and, beyond measure, to Sian, for the years; and for raising my Spirits.

Contents

For those beyond the curtain

Punch

Master of the Revels

We have two doors furnishing access to the stage.
Entrances and exits are equally difficult.
The wardrobe mistress will, for a small fee,
assist you with cap, bells,
traditional daubs of apoplectic rouge.
Just before your cue
the props master will hand your bludgeon-
he has jurisdiction here.
Trust him to know all that is required.
On stage use your own judgement.

Remember, they expect a good show:
misrule pays handsomely.
We've only one law:
avoid eyes and intimate parts-
all else is fodder.
Should any scene be overplayed
some wounds can be dressed
but skill and time are limited.
No prompts will be necessary.

Justly proud of our scenery
modelled on works by Caravaggio,
we strive for a passionate reality.
In these circumstances some damage is inevitable:
breakages must be paid for
though all characters are replaceable.

Consider too how advantageous
judicious use of the mirror can be,
or other facilities-
someone of your stature
cannot afford to be taken short.

An audience of innocents, lovers,
pimps, charlatans, mendicants
and criminals awaits.
They must labour under a sweated knavery
if they are to be made to pay.
Hasten, so as not to disappoint.

One word; above all,
In all things, at all costs,
Remember your dignity.

Punch confronts the demons

Before each performance
Punch hatches stratagems to outwit Death—
Jack Ketch's noose, the severing jaws;
weighs his cudgel for another bout
he knows will earn him earfuls
from the doctor, the skeleton, the man in blue.

The planet runs its summer axis.
Chaos and Chronos are his trade.
He must dance to the pipe, beat his little drum
and every time the chill bites deeper.
By what dark authority should he endure
the clawing in his guts,
that wild expression, hump back, hook nose,
call for blood? Still, he spits on his palms,
butchering the dramatis personae.

His cackle echoes—
beneath him, in the tiny theatre,
he hears the devil cough and curse
and mount the stairs—
all other matters must be adjourned;
feels the rising heat,
scours memory for one good deed to
 save him.

Gladiatorial, he's roused:
he'll be the paradigm and picture of the age.

Sans hope sans faith there's only rage.

Punch assays the virginals

Sometimes he wakes and thinks he is in love.

Through the darkness
the puppet master's daughter converses with angels—
unearthly wordless sounds.

Thin white fingers induce arpeggios, scales,
she rocks to rhythms, scans a secret script—
her music conjures elsewheres.

He tries the keys
but does not have the trick of it—
mysteries a bludgeoning can't unfurl.

Could he summon the actors now,
all earthly discord would be resolved—
his body forgets its bruises when she plays.

He is haunted by memories of the dark,
fumes of glue, shavings, brushes propped in pots—
alarm as his features emerge under the whittling knife.

And beyond—a time of strange music of leaves and feathers,
shrill pipings at dawn, the green forest floor—
the tree, cracked bark, the axe.

Punch unhap

It was like this. Grey tides, after a poor excuse of a journey. Radiances, cold shores, loud music, dirty streets and fishermen casting lines in hard dawn light; salt rime in my clothes, everywhere blazons demanding rapid intimate exchanges. Weather report despatched as per expectation, ditto views on another's absence. I stay safe in my little tent, emerging for short performances. Little profit in it. Children laugh or cry at my excesses. It's all the same to me.

An off night. Then out to the creeping crawlers publife.

In and out. Come and go. Oranges and Lemons. Cash tinkle girl. She's quick. Beating the machine in skirt and heels. My lucky night except for the rough she's with. Feeding the slot.

He's at her

Apple. Orange. Hold.

How much will you pay me … I'll give you five farthings … I'll give you What for

Apple. Apple. Nudge. Spin. Bitter lemon. Not tempted.

Try my luck. Apple. Orange. Lemon. Hopeless. He's leery all over her. Getting late. The music loud. She press-hold-nudges and cash tinkles like her laughter, silver-streaming into her lucky bag. So now she's packing up, smirk cold-shouldering this slouch in piss-scented denims. Last coin. The old lady gave me for helping her cross the street. Nudge nudge no pay. Kick the machine. My hand up its innards, groping for a refund. Deus exit machina: landlord's special exit out the back on my arse. No moon so into the dark go we. Can't see a can't feel a one step two step. Mob flashlight in among the silvery bins. Witness the fall. Sweet sorrowful music. She's laid out. Where's the dignity, I want to know. Can't you keep your clothes to yourself? Shambles of a cloth yard, blood everywhere, a blade shaft hilted in her ribs. Scatter of needles bright in the torchlight. His boots, alley echoing, tramping off, cursing her foul names, her purse gutted. No sign of Old Bill though I do offer.

No point, she says, done for. Unlucky in love. For fuck's sake. What song's that? A way out after all now you see me now you can't you speak to me when I'm looking at you there's you and me the quick and the you're the last thing for once pretend sooner or later you mean it before the music stops just once hold shut up hold and kiss me quick

Punch appeals to the Eumenides

A complaint!
Justice, O spawn of blood!
Justice from those who steal my character
and break me with sticks and stones,
rend my vestments and deck me in drollery.
See how they have carved my flesh into cruel distortion.
Pursue them and make them know
the pains of age,
its ebb and drift,
the agonies of loss.

Accused under false law,
compelled by the conceit of others,
I speak only with malicious voices,
enact their crimes,
practise their deceits
and pursue their vices,
for which I receive much praise.

Hunt them through their temples and high offices.
Let their secrets and bribes be as hot coals to scorch their palms.
Those that would make me the instrument of their decisions,
gather armies in my name,
befoul the streets and scourge the poor.
The crimes they lay upon me
pierce like thorns upon my brow.

My life is not my own,
but living death by another's hand.

Holy ones,
friends to the wronged,
grant me vengeance

or restore my innocence.

Punch's descent into the labyrinth

Neither to right nor left
always down —

He counted the levels,
at first he recognised faces—
none spoke—
bent on survival,
crowds saw plague or a certain doom,
washed past,
then complications-
only his shadow leading or following
and empty galleries
reminiscent of an earlier path.
At those times he could not recall
one good reason for his journey,
the thread of memory slackening;
sometimes he thought he knew where he was-
once he met one like himself
who, challenged, turned his back and wept,
till at last he thought he was getting close—
voices round the next corner,
intimacies, laughter, conversation—

he readied his stick.

Punch and the unexamined life

Then again I wake to heat
and looming faces,
the echo of voices distant and strange.
No physic for this:
it is time to crack skulls, wrestle with unearthly forces.
I am always victorious, but do not know why.
Who am I to argue?
I do my job. If the sun is bright I close an eye.

They receive rage as a gift: or an entitlement
sacrosanct as wine and bread.
Applause is like a threat of worlds to come.
After the beatings and killings I hear their laughter.
They do not understand that the play is not entertainment.
We must omit all passionate weeping.
To them we figure only the useful dead.

I overhear conversations. One said to another once
that from the top of the first tree he climbed
he could see further than he had ever been.
He returned to the ground changed irrevocably.

Better stay put.
Nothing is worth such a catastrophe.

Goya: Duel with Cudgels

As far as can be determined
these are the last;
though conditions are far from ideal,
it shouldn't take long.
Bogged to the knees,
the blood coursing already,
their fragmented flesh will soon
colour the bleak landscape.
Now carrion creatures gather.
Still they lay it on.
Like exhausted drunks,
they labour at each other's despair.
Their sweat and grunts ignite more fury,
Muscles pulped by the thud of cudgels,
they're flayed to the guts,
shit long ago thrashed out.
Soon the white gleam of bones
must be exposed in moonlight.
Even that won't satisfy
until ribs and shanks are pulverised
for wind to find
and marrow runs in slurry.
As stars rotate,
they are silhouettes of exhausted men
breaking stones in the workhouse,
struggling with impossible burdens
to purchase mean crusts and sleep.
The torment is endless.
Still they must endure.
The decree is clear:
Throughout the wide ranged kingdoms,
when only one man stands,
dying but undefeated
and nothing else remains,
may peace descend on the land.

Punch at the opera

This cracked falsetto means I'm type cast.
For years I coveted better roles.
Eventually fell in with Pagliacci's mob.
Now and then I skip a shift, get lost in La Boheme,
applauding the tubercular cough, the exquisite death.
It's light relief watching tragic pawns,
or snoring through some half-baked plot
about triumphs of human nature.
But before the end sense stirrings in my gut-
especially in Der Rosenkavalier:
Lightly clasp and freely release;
Those who do not so
are punished by life.

And this is comic opera.

All I'm saying

Should we ever meet
there are free tickets to my show.

The Perilous Question

Right on cue, just as we're about to start,
she comes to take me aside.
Her brood's left under firm instruction.

Navigating sun hats and dropped cornets,
she constantly looks back, treading on toes.

I withdraw from this familiar scenario:
her sunken-eyed, sleepless visage.
In these symptoms I am skilled as a plague doctor.

I know better than to come out.
They think because they've seen a thing or two
they can work you. I've seen more.

Just present a portion of myself;
my huge proboscis droops quizzically through drapes.
Let her grieve on that.

She's shifty, looking around.
Full of parental dignitas, demanding reassurance
it will be an *appropriate* show.

I know what's coming. Sotto voce,
the question of the centuries:
Do you do the hanging?

I am nothing if not consistent, in principle
and discretion. I've had her sort on her knees.
Madame, for certain: we aim to please.

Amateur Dramatics

He beats his tiny spoon upon the board.
He cannot be kept waiting.
He has rights.
They should run to serve his whims.
He searches for his stick —
he will teach them respect.
He bawls and hollers.
He will have justice.
Is he not the one for whom sunlit hordes gather
to laugh and gape and shriek?
He hears the scatter of coins.
but they serve him slops or bread and milk
discarding him with life's detritus
to await dramas of appeasement in one act

He has strange thoughts
of nights of bread and wine,
enraptured crowds.
Tired of acting his character
he remembers tender hands,
the scent of nard.

Slow handclap.
Drapes.

The Revels

Grip

Climb the teachers said so hand over hand
barefoot in vest and shorts rope trick up
                                        to nowhere

and played out topping hands over and above
maddening by turns to slaps
                                        then fists

but an invalid carriage I saw once
muscled along the kerbside the crank going hand
                                        over hand

its black cloak straining shoulders bat winged
and couldn't ungrip seeing's quicksand drag
                                        of gravity

or unlearn the implacable formula
of effort against gains and
                                        that time

watching her fingers curl on the parapet
but seeing the flow and not
                                        reaching out

and the slow labour of years and the forgetting
until the new maths of each
                                        curtailed step

balancing hot angles through hip and wrist
and gauging the weight
                                        and cost

hand over hand of each release
grab halt and
                breath

at each chairback table edge hand hold
towards somewhere
                        the pictures

Convalescence

Post-op she qualified for special treatment:
convalescent home, sea air. We visited weekends.
She made excuses for the tasteless food.
Everyone wore brave faces.

Through drizzle we scoured the front.
Dank. End of season. No good.
We tried a shelter near some toilets.
The wind cut in. Someone had been sick.

A lame mongrel followed us,
pulsing turds between peeling beech huts.
We shooed it. *Go home boy.* She said,
People might think it belongs. Our crap.

Down an alley it turned out scrofulous cats,
sank between two bins for the night.
We sensed the last of it, black tongue, wheezing breath,
a cold burden stiffening on the morning.

We found a Punch and Judy man setting up
off the pier, a cheaper pitch.
He spied custom: there was no escape.
So we shivered on wet benches.

The afternoon dealt out judgements
of an implacable deity. Gullible victims—
the hangman garrotted in his own cruel loop,
the bobby buffoon—deserved their suffering.

We stalled in the pageantry of violence.
Torture, death, abuse
passed off with start-eyed circumventions
against the mirthless cackles,

until it dawned, sometime between the misfortune
of the baby in the mincer
and the sausage guts spilling out,
she could stand no more and had made an early exit.

We found her in the municipal gardens.
She told us red was predominant.
At some point the rain almost stopped.
We had not paid.
                    All of which
cheered us up no end.

lost poem

something about a bridge a meeting
day melting into evening
the river's unquelled reflection

strands of memory
twining through the pale wash of sky
figures emerging through torsions of perspective

an exchange of words touch
and steps echoing on stones
a haunting of objects

if not this then ambient light
and colours of the way someone saw this once

something about the reflection
and stones echoing words across lapping water

the callousness of flights of birds
as ripples fragment their passing
and from an open window drift of a nocturne

and landscape focusing the unlimited self
as poem and loneliness
or conversation with distance

and more lucid the stones mirrored
and curious lift of the arches the antique lamps
stars pointing the dark flow

and the departures that are something about
the one who leaves creating the one who stays

and how words transform figures at nightfall
into more than silhouettes

and always about letting go
and getting it back our own way

it might have been something about love
or its awakening or your arms' reach against emptiness
or breath and the warmth of flesh

or how the thought finds the word
or the pain as breeze stirs her hair

and something about becoming
and remote and strange integrities
and unreality merging with the fact

Bergamask for the Neoplatonists

Any attempt to describe 'the Good' would be ... to include it among the beings to which 'thus' is applicable.

Plotinus, trans John Gregory in The Neoplatonists

how they sustained it
put on music
sat it out in pairs
straightened pillows dead-headed flowers
and hid the husks
                as connections crumbled
wetting cracked lips
trying not to hear
the secret resentments
desperate and mouthing
in shoals like poisoned fish

and never fully readied for
out of nowhere shards of clarity
and the twitch of fingers in tempo
that meant she still harboured options
on spring's full throated outbursts

but it was over sooner
separated only by otherness
from the red blink of the cd's zero

to salve the news we unstacked shelves
cleared corners
dusted off and played old vinyls all afternoon
slipped back through the jazz age
outside was sleet
street lights glossed its yellow melt
and that was all

but come night's renderings
to assert the good
in the redeemed space
like this you said
and tried to teach me what you learned
in dance class
                    we steered clear
laughed off my clod-footed tripped beat
mis-step wrong turns
                              and
paused in hold
through the weighted silence between each track
thought what it is to move
among the beings where song prevails
and perfect abstracts still apply

Augury

the quickening click of heels
laughter and screams vent the nightclub bars
perfumed doorway congregations
migrate to other sides of town
through a thousand scents
and visions of half-lit night

pale rushes in the current
or braced, arms entwined
outflow
colour and light
flowering on grey pavements

secret-laden bags, shaded iphones
in dangerous caress
hot cars' engines
rev and race
        and all this
time
open to persuasion
unconvinced

birdflights westering
catch love's cry
early navigators

but nothing
lies beyond here
at the wave chill's edge
        still
frail feathered their certainty drives at moonlit oceans
their journeyings quarter the sky
resolute
backs to the receding land

silently their reasons gather
                                  as
loose formations close in
like mottling
on
skin thinning on this hand

tattoo parlour: midnight

the bells' epiphany
quickens an Aphrodite
through backways neon's nightscape
the faded charities
shuttered for dark

shared playlists
navigate her purpose
where barred displays
engaged to sell her gold for cash
secretively blink

she seeks just form
a codex for unique scripts
of her fantasy
her intent messaging
harbours new passwords

at crossings
figments in huddled congress
from lamp to lamp
crowd to Acheron
through the shadow time

by the river's transgressions
of scud and foam
she celebrates the flood
the upturned supermarket cart
the silk caress of underwear

discards without pain
the glance that locks
then slides the body's length
to calculate
the passing trade

glimpsed alabaster curves through glass
charged ranks of cosmetics
immaculate statuary
art of us
scorch ashen memory

stilt-heeled escapes
the sirens' insistence
perfumes from doorways
of pooled lie
to plead the breathless crisis

fashion this impermanence
make holy this form for us
and at the latent hour tell
in the minding of love's design upon this thigh
the urgent story

Latecomer

Ave atque vale.
                    Catullus 101

You surprised us
coming so late,
enduring that brief term;
we had thought all that long past.

We took fragments in a plastic bag.
The doctor picking over pink and grey,
could determine nothing clear. We left you there.
Somewhere out the back an incinerator hummed.

If I ever find a religion
it will rehearse subjunctives,
observing transmigration of the soul,
that I might in another's grasp or look
sense the smart of recognition
                            or that you
may find ease among the Ancients;
perhaps with Catullus,
who, far-travelled over desolate seas,
too late at a death,
although denied greeting or farewell,
stays

urging poetry from his grief.

The mermaid in Fresno

A woman found wandering in Fresno near San Francisco was unable to provide a name or address. She claimed to be a mermaid. When examined, she was found to have webbed toes.

I

the sea that could not finish her
the crested shoals
nowhere among her kind

her one demand
Does King Alexander live?
satisfied only

with oblations
and courteous lies
He lives and reigns and conquers the world

there are complications
among the sorrows of those she wrecks
she keeps secret

the day he bathed her hair
and pain of hot stone
searing the webs between her toes

she bears the salt sting
going among us
praising immortals

II

they require an identity
a matter of importance to them
why these foolish questions
again she cites the sorority of Thessalonike
abiding in sea caves

why persist and never comprehend
the secretive curl of weed at the shore
or question land's preoccupation
with the stoop of foolish gulls
the melodrama of grey waves

they will have their answer
her hair stirs
            wind rises
closer the beat
      of pounding surf

cries of the lost

III

she is drowning
and unable to die
step by step

will regain her element
twilit streets down to sand
trace who she might be

curious prints of toes
spread and blur with each wave
foam blanched weed and solitary rock

image the groves of her dead
the spume's shock
and impulse between her thighs

webs blossoming to the salt
the flow drawing her hair
and green falling light are visitations

hails and knows them
for songs though anguished
that thread and plume the tide

Caravaggio battles with the leaves

these days we go armed
a peasant arsenal
of sacks and besoms
where dead things kick up
demon sediment and leavings
cities erupt with chaos
the green world splits
in secret regenerations
       its credo
by the cartload
as though all labour were
shovellings of light
      each morning
our reversals are complete
the day's work lost under layers

chiaroscuro through remnant boughs
"a foul and rotten member"
from each wreck
he chased them down
to palm just one
before it grounded
      incessantly
as if by any breeze
casually
their uplift mastery of air
stalls
to one outcome
—for here they must dwell—
the wind's rape
charged powers of light
on flesh
    through the rot-down
— this short tenure
folly
their flight endless—

still life a madness
or cause to kill a man
                         but
distanced to the canvas' edge
their living green aches
a delicacy beyond touch
                         this
is how a man seeks pardon
their grieving derangements
a starling cloud alighting
rags of summer's shade
all entreat—

intimately though we observe the scene—

Pass tenderly amongst the fallen
those radiant obscure
the sleeping Virgin
the trickster mob
the Baptist's head
his lamb his spear
                    for these
envisioned shroudless
have much to bear

—softly lest they stir—

Hunters in the Snow: Pieter Bruegel the Elder

What do they search for
these hunters in the snow
returning with exhausted dogs and shouldered spears
empty handed to a place where ponds lie frozen
and starving birds dip over skating villagers?
Look, a figure hurries across the bridge with news
towards the fire's glow
under a pallid sun.

Something ended in these fields and forests
while they were gone-
Now the lean winter stretches out
grey shadows of elongated trees
like bones.
Had it been a bracelet, brooch, a lover's jewel
fallen among the bleak boughs of the dark year's lapse
spring would uncover it:
                              but for this there is no cure.

plainchant

divergent narratives
old loves' censure in city lights
still the achievable pathways beckoning
past wash of shingle and receding tide
the reshaping unending
                            to wake to this
in the dead eyes unredeemed

The birds consider their madness

Landscape is uncertain
so our attire is bright rags and ashes
as if to alight momentarily.
Balancing the tip of a cathedral in my claw
I feel stone turn to ruin.
This was not my intention.
Far below
a young woman mouths and waves her arms.
She would tell us something
that only perspective reveals:
her heart beats
but the mind is frail.
Once she was one of us.

Bloodied feathers in the thorn brake
solitude of olive groves
until the gods in pity transformed her.
Now each day she practises to be
more adept
to laugh alone, sing alone;
leave, like us, no imprint where she slept;
through prayer and self-reproach
studies to regain the power of flight,
to navigate the air's unreason;

says All landscape is a problem of scale.
Observant how fields' and forests' unrest
changes at our song,
to forsake our history
she calls us down with crumbs to a table.
This beckoning unsettles us.
She cannot last long.

The birds dispute with Aquinas

After the solstice
the declining sun casts longer shadows.
Though natural, from Aristotle's rudiments
to desire a favoured oblivion,
or frame infinity to human shape,
your primum mobile carries no force here.

Concede desire to figure in the temporal air,
set something down,
though had he asked us, we could have posited how
pure song defines us;
witness the flight of those
who do not require the soul,
remote purposes perfected though obscure.
At evening, remark
our soaring paths through lengthening shade.

Aubade: the birds consider human desire

Onsets seep into the horizon,
shift the dark upwards,
a shroud unsettling
constantly elsewhere.
This should be our time of song.
Cold benisons of light
ghost-form
only long enough to say
Though we might once have loved
It is not enough.
                We recognise
through black-twigged winters
what's acquired when our agony rises,
migratory, febrile:
a look of enforcements-
desire, escape, a life becoming.
Then words:
If our departure causes pain
it is our own.
Thus the appeasement of guilt.
Thus
the defrayal of grief.

There are memories
in shell fragments,
the twig and leaf sediment of the nest,
faint residues of nurture.
Snow finds tiny bodies
feather stiff.
From here on
our naked skeletons
make flutes of bone and air.
At day's allocation
Our chorus:

        More and more
song seems just breath.
More and more
Love's celebrations feel like death.

Standing stone

the OS *Position of antiquity*
lapses in scrub and moorland
we expected gods

border country
poised in two kingdoms
braced in loyalties

in muted conclaves
the long shafted spears reversed
trading concessions

slaves and weeping daughters
cattle and skins
the price of peace

is a shadow
traversing the tundra
missing nothing

its terrain the rule of talons
the small death under the outcrop
and distant fires

through rain's investiture
of sanctioned weighted solitudes

withstanding

Metamorphosis

To be sure it is ended
make inroads;

carve out the heart
of the dead community,

disjoint frame by frame
skull, wing, thorax,

and test noon's silence
for resonance.

Sisters of Phaeton,
your amber tears

confirm the tiny labours of gatherers
in sloughs of wax,

and in the resignation
of frozen arcadians

find seed the weight of dust,
the eye's grit.

www.ingramcontent.com/pod-product-compliance
Lightning Source LLC
Chambersburg PA
CBHW020442030426
42337CB00014B/1356